Rakesh Weds Nature

All are invited – to celebrate the union of love and life.

Rakesh Chandra Kumar

India | USA | UK

Copyright © Rakesh Chandra Kumar
All Rights Reserved.

This book has been self-published with all reasonable efforts taken to make the material error-free by the author. No part of this book shall be used, reproduced in any manner whatsoever without written permission from the author, except in the case of brief quotations embodied in critical articles and reviews.

The Author of this book is solely responsible and liable for its content including but not limited to the views, representations, descriptions, statements, information, opinions, and references ["Content"]. The Content of this book shall not constitute or be construed or deemed to reflect the opinion or expression of the Publisher or Editor. Neither the Publisher nor Editor endorse or approve the Content of this book or guarantee the reliability, accuracy, or completeness of the Content published herein and do not make any representations or warranties of any kind, express or implied, including but not limited to the implied warranties of merchantability, fitness for a particular purpose.

The Publisher and Editor shall not be liable whatsoever...

Made with ❤ on the BookLeaf Publishing Platform
www.bookleafpub.in
www.bookleafpub.com

Dedication

To

All whom I have met,
And all whom I have not yet met.
In your joys and sorrows, I find my own;
In your struggles, you are not alone.
On life's long path, from start to end,
I shall walk with you as a noble friend.
This poetry collection springs from your inspiration;
Please accept my humble dedication.

Preface

Rakesh Weds Nature — in this poetry collection, I try to capture all my intimate moments with Nature.

A poet is always married to his inspiration, and my inspiration has always been Nature. Hence, the title *Rakesh Weds Nature*. For me, Nature is not just the trees, rivers, blue sky, clouds that an artist paints or a photographer captures — though these aspects bring me immense joy. Nature, for me, holds a much deeper meaning: the laws that govern and sustain all life.

I understand that the line between reality and fantasy is a fine line. In life, one often feels tempted to lean towards fantasy. Yet, I do not intend to live in a dreamland, chasing illusory inspiration. I find solace and fulfillment in reality, as it manifests from moment to moment.

The central idea of this poetry collection is **self-discovery**. Though the poems trace my journey through the maze of life, I believe many readers will find echoes of their own struggles here. From experience, I know that those who genuinely seek to know the purpose of life will realize it — with persistent effort and the support of like-minded people.

I enjoy writing poems with rhyme. There is no fixed structure to my poetry, and I do not claim deep knowledge of poetic craft. I simply try to thread words together to express an experience or inspiration arising in my mind.

I began writing to give form to emotions triggered by my interactions with the people around me.

The poem *"Woman is Nature"* was my reaction to assaults on women. *"Love Sans Lust"* responded to the rising number of divorces. Both, I feel, are wounds of our times.
"Right Time to Marry" and *"Right Intention to Marry"* arose from the questions people often ask me — *When are you getting married?* and *Why not yet?*

"Flying Out of Mom's Nest" was born from an exchange with my mother, and *"Noble Friendship"* after an argument with a friend. *"Nature's Fury"* and *"When Humanity Strays"* reflect my response to urban floods, global conflicts, and even the treatment of stray dogs.

"All For One, One for All," *"The Child Within Her Wrinkles,"* and *"To Sir, With Love"* are the expressions of

my gratitude toward my mother, grandmother, aunt, and mentor.

"Could She Be the One?" is about the wonderful women I once proposed to, and *"Till I Break Free"* was written with a woman in mind, who was struggling with heartbreak from a past relationship.

"My Romance With Nature" emerged from my trekking experience in the Kodachadri Hills. *"Nature's Blanket"* reflects the feeling that though we all are different, we rest on Nature's lap (the Earth) under Nature's blanket (the sky).

"The Rise Within" draws an analogy between a rocket launch and our spiritual ascent.

"Awakening to Life" explores sensitivity toward a newborn.

"The Adventure That's Parenting" appreciates parents who sacrifice their comfort to raise a human being — a noble act worthy, I feel, of a Nobel Prize.

Finally, *"My Passionate Quest — Discovering Her Laws,"* *"In Tune with Nature's Law,"* and *"The Ultimate Journey — Beyond Nature"* capture my inner quest, which I lovingly reveal to the readers.

All these poems are born from the inspiration of the people around me. Some teach us how to live; others, how not to. In a way, everyone is a teacher — a mentor in disguise.

I invite you, my reader and guest, to take a tour through my mind —my true home. After all, we do not truly live in houses, mansions, or bungalows; we live in our minds. It is therefore important to keep the mind pure and light.

In the context of this collection, my mind is a wedding venue — where *Rakesh Weds Nature*.
I warmly welcome you to this celebration; may you find pleasant surprises within.

I sincerely hope that all people live happily and peacefully, with a sense of purpose.

— Rakesh Chandra Kumar

Acknowledgements

I would like to express my deepest gratitude to my parents for their love and sacrifice, and for giving me the gift of life. I honor their struggles in raising me, knowing it was never easy. At times, I hesitate to embrace marriage, considering the challenges of raising a child. Nevertheless, I find courage in the thought that if my parents could do it, then perhaps I can too.

I am grateful to my teachers for their affection and guidance, and I have always held them in high regard.

I cherish the support of my friends, who remain ever dear to me. I thank my friend, Sai Chinmay (from Kasaragod), who encouraged me to write poems.

I acknowledge with respect the wisdom of my mentors, especially Mr. John Hemanth Kumar, whose guidance continues to walk with me on this journey of life.

    I am also grateful to BookLeaf Publishing for the TheWriteAngle writing challenge initiative, which inspired me to publish my poetry collection.

Woman is Nature

A Woman as Fire:
The nature of fire is always to burn,
Of women, so must a man learn.
She guides the wise to their heart's desire,
But fools she consumes in her blazing pyre.

A Woman as Water:
The nature of water is to bind,
And this, in woman, a man must find.
She holds the wise with her gentle grace,
But for fools, she washes away their trace.

A Woman as Earth:
The nature of earth is to nourish,
In women, this truth will flourish.
She feeds the wise with food to relish,
But fools she starves till they perish.

A Woman as Air:
The nature of air is ever to move,

Worthy of her love, a man must prove.
She offers the wise a cooling breeze,
But fools she sends a blizzard to freeze.

Therefore,
A woman is Nature,
A vast and fertile field.
A man is a farmer,
Reaping what life will yield.

The wise man sows seeds of love,
And reaps a life abundant and bright.
The fool sows seeds of lust,
And lives in a state of plight.

Love Sans Lust

Where there is lust, there is no love,
For lust and hate work hand in glove.
They stand as two sides of one coin,
Binding our energy to the groin.

A man who truly loves his woman,
Never will he waste his semen.
To conceive a child is his intention,
Not mere desire or blind copulation.

Marriages are blessed in heaven,
Yet no single key to success is given.
Lust is surely not one of the ways,
For it runs with hate in the mind's maze.

To Sir, With Love

Dear John Sir (my friend and mentor),

You comfort me like a teddy bear,
And show tough love like a grizzly bear.
When I am troubled by life's miseries,
And find it hard to unravel life's mysteries,
I pray to the universe:
"Please send a friend with whom I can converse."
And there you are, listening to me,
No matter how silly my questions may be.
I am always grateful for your time and presence,
And I strive to emulate your forbearance.
Wherever life takes you in the cycle of birth and death,
I hope to find you — to honor my debt of gratitude
By being present, breath after breath.

Right Time to Marry

Got a job and earning one's bread,
Isn't the right time to tie the sacred thread.

Saved some money and flaunting the bling,
Isn't the right time to offer a wedding ring.

Started a business and turned worldly wise,
Isn't the right time to utter *kubul* thrice.

Friends got married and settled indeed,
Isn't the right time to sign the marriage deed.

One is happy with life — single or married,
It's the right time to choose someone,
who'll weep when you're buried.

Right Intention to Marry

When was marriage conceptualized?
Was it when man became civilized?
A few, because of marriage, feel petrified—
Is it due to the way it is glorified?

A truth about marriage we must admit:
It is for love and sex — not a license or permit.
Let us not rush to pacify our urges,
Lest we end up holding lifelong grudges.

Elders want to sustain the bloodline,
And set for the young a daunting timeline.
Many who fail to meet that deadline,
Choose the live-in model as a lifeline.

It is expensive now to raise a child,
With school fees driving one wild.
Many, choosing instead to adopt a pet,
Avoid falling into the well of debt.

Yet, I wish to see people get married,
And live together, never worried,
Let them choose to conceive the divine,
And put the brakes on humanity's decline.

Nature's Fury

Trees fell, buildings stood,
Nature bled, none understood.

Lakes dried, plots laid,
No heed to her was paid.

Garbage dumped, drains choked,
None listened when she croaked.

Glaring at Man's wicked games,
She waited to make her claims.

She summoned the storm,
Unleashing her furious form.

The raging deluge
Had people run for refuge.

The human race came to a halt,
By Nature's timed, deadly assault.

Nature's Blanket

Another day has passed,
Filling a new page in life's diary.
Like any other day —
A rollercoaster ride, enjoyed not fully.

Everyone stepped out to meet their duties,
Marching toward their destinies.
We remain sane, thanks to Nature—
She offers her therapy freely.

We all sleep under the same black sky,
Adorned with stars shining with all their might.
Hoping for a bright and happy tomorrow,
We smile and wish all a warm good night.

The Rise Within

A rocket standing on Earth,
Serves no purpose, holds no worth.
It must burn its fuel in brevity,
To overcome Earth's gravity.
It undergoes staged separation,
Detaching its parts in a fierce explosion.
It puts the satellite in space,
And completes its task with grace.

Likewise, a man must strive —
Not only to survive, but to thrive.
He's got to burn emotions that are heavy,
And rise above all that's topsy-turvy.
He must undergo transformation,
Through detachment born of realization.
Only then can he reach that stage,
Forever free from the mind's cage.

When Humanity Strays

The entire world is
Engulfed in war;
The air is filled with hatred,
Wide and far.

As a result,
City folks seek an end
To the stray dogs —
once man's best friend.

I wonder where we're heading,
With all this mass beheading;
Killing each other and fellow beings,
Inconsiderate of others' feelings.

We all have a choice:
To love all and rejoice,
Come, let us live in harmony —
The greatest gift to our progeny.

All for One, One for All

My mother loves me a lot,
Says I am the one she sought.

She knocked upon the temple doors,
Performed her rites and sacred chores.

She prayed for a child divine,
Who would love all and shine.

In her arms she held a baby boy,
Who relished in her smile and joy.

I was her world, yet not her luck —
She worked so hard and sometimes felt stuck.

So she sought help from my granny,
Who kindly agreed to be my nanny.

She also sought my aunt's help,
Who made sure I never had to yelp.

So I grew up under these women's care,
They protected me with love so rare.

Life was not smooth for anyone,
Yet I could feel love from everyone.

My childhood was peaceful and sweet,
Their care made every day complete.

How can I ever repay this debt of gratitude?
If I'm happy today, it's because of their attitude.

The only way to repay is to share my happiness,
Yet distance sometimes strengthens togetherness.

Flying Out of Mom's Nest

Once I told my mom, "I'm done with my studies,
I wish to work and earn like my buddies."
She said, "Nothing doing – you better do higher studies,
For the brides are all smart, have you seen their CVs?"

Then I told my mom,
"I'm not ready for marriage.
I'd rather go to the Himalayas
And befriend a sage."

She said,
"Yeah, in your dreams!
You sit and watch your breath?
You plan to leave this house –
You may, after my death."

I said, "Mom, this so unfair,
Career and marriage are my own affair."
She said, "I'm your mother,
I know what's good for you.

You're far too innocent –
Of this world, you have no clue."

I pleaded, "Mom, please let me be,
I'm no longer a boy; I wish to be free."
She wept and said, "You'll understand a mother's heart,
When you're a father and when your child tears you apart.

I empathized with her – in life she'd had little fun.
I asked, "Do you wish to live with an unhappy son?"
Doing a routine job for a fixed salary,
And buying his wife, each month, a saree?"

Mom takes a pause, but never gives up.
I stay calm, lest she flares up.
Mom, may peace rest within your chest –
I cannot forever live in your nest.

Till I Break Free

Yes, I am depressed –
Yet, I choose to smile,
Because it makes me look good,
At least for a while.

I go through waves of emotion,
Feels like a rollercoaster ride.
Listen to me as I share my pain –
For I need someone to guide.

I suppress my emotions –
Surfing on a stormy tide.
I can't always act so tough;
Would it help me if I cried?

I sit alone in the corner of my room,
Hoping someone will help me bloom.
To tell me I am still beloved,
And accept me – a puzzle unsolved.

Just sit beside me and mind your thing;
If I need you, I'll ask for something.
A pat on my head, a kiss on my cheek –
Anything gentle that doesn't make me weak.

Never push me out of depression,
For that only breeds suspicion –
On your love and acceptance for me.
Have patience – wait till I break free.

Could She Be the One?

A young lady, worthy of praise,
I knew her smile from my school days.
She was indeed my very first crush,
And often left me with a blush.
I thought we could be there for each other,
But she got married – to some big brother.

Another lady, smiling with her gaze,
Came into my life like a fierce blaze.
In haste, she took my number,
And woke me up from my slumber.
I believed her to be the one,
But she got married – and had a son.

Another lady, with divine grace,
Walked past me at a steady pace.
While meditating on the light in her heart,
She wore a smile that defied all art.
That smile that day took me by shock,
And years later, I asked her for wedlock.

She said she has someone in her life,
And wished me good luck in my strife.

My parents keep running to the marriage broker,
Lest I end up like Raj Kapoor – in the movie *Mera Naam Joker*.

Yet when I see a smile on someone,
I ask myself – "Could she be the one?"

Awakening to Life

He was pushed from within
And pulled out,
Made to lie beside her —
Who hosted him day in and day out.

Everyone cheered him
With smiles, kisses, and tears of joy,
Unaware of what he had been through,
All rushed to hold him as if he were a toy.

A huge task lies ahead of him:
To make sense of what he sees and feels,
So he can smile at those who smiled
And spread happiness with all life reveals.

The Child Within Her Wrinkles

She was old and wise,
And I – the apple of her eyes.

She was not just a grandmother –
A teacher, a guide, and a mother.

Work was her worship,
She lived a life full of hardship.

To save a penny, she'd walk a mile,
But never once forgot to smile.

She was old and wise,
A child in wrinkled skin guise.

I picture her grey hair and broken teeth,
Her splendid smile she did bequeath.

She told her tales of virtue with ease,

And left us pleading – "Once more, Amma, please."

A wonderful woman I've come across so far,
Though she's no more, she'll always be my superstar.

Noble friendship

My friends don't like advice,
They'd rather embrace any vice.
I exercise restraint in my speech,
Lest they drift beyond my reach.

I feel like speaking of my pain,
Not wishing ever to be their bane.
I do not wish to impose my will,
Though I may err in goodwill.

The journey of life is long,
Forgive me, but don't take me wrong.
I value open conversation,
Backbiting only stirs frustration.

There's no time for us to fight,
We're aging under time's might.
To help us sail through life's hardship,
There awaits a ship — our noble friendship.

My Romance with Nature

Trees, waterfalls, and birds on the hills
Beckon me — I test my hiking skills.
Green meadows and streams pass by,
As I climb toward the summit high.

Clouds rally over the hills and weep,
Shooting raindrops into valleys deep.
The rays of light that pierce right through,
Make me pause and wonder — what a view!

Lush greenery spreads all around,
With flowers bright, Nature is crowned.
I dream of a small hut in this place,
To live with a woman embodying grace.

The hills, like her bosoms, it seems,
Oozing with springs that flow as streams.
We drink Nature's milk with grateful hands,
And pray that wisdom in us withstands.

I realize that I've strayed too long,
In an illusory world where I don't belong.
It is time to ground my wandering thoughts,
And set my mind free —untying the knots.

An Adventure That's Parenting

Dear parents,

I hope this poem finds you well,
Please know that in my heart you dwell.
I write to express my admiration,
For your courage and determination.

Raising a child is no child's play,
May you stay strong — I sincerely pray.
Freedom, social life, and sleepless nights,
Are sacrifices of unbounded heights.

I understand the pain couples go through,
To conceive a baby — in a test tube grew.
Unfathomable is the plight of parents,
Who give birth to children with impairments.

There'll be people who take you for a ride,
And schools that say, "Admission denied."

No matter the hardships that may come,
Keep marching to the beat of your drum.

The world needs people who remain sane,
If we wish to see humanity sustain.
Trust me, your efforts won't go in vain —
In your children, as inspiration, you remain.

My Passionate Quest — Discovering Her Laws

As a curious child, I asked my grandmother,
"Granny, why do people get married to each other?"
She said,
"Son, it is to continue the family bloodline.
It is our destiny, designed by the divine."

As a restless teenager, I kept daydreaming,
And hunted for *pleasure* in online streaming.
I witnessed how the mind got corrupted,
As dormant lust from deep within erupted.

As a young adult, I saw a ball of light enter me;
And set me upon a course-correction spree.
The burden of past actions weighed upon me —
I was on my knees, pleading to break free.

The churning of the mind's ocean was at full steam;
Helplessly, I kept drifting to either extreme.
The energy within was either expressed or suppressed —

That it could be transmuted, I'd never guessed.

Napoleon Hill, in *Think and Grow Rich,*
Writes about sex transmutation — a mystical switch.
That was inspiring, and I gave it a try,
But theory without practice leaves one high and dry.

At the peak of my spiritual yearning,
There came a moment — truly life-turning.
I sat cross-legged, eyes closed, for ten days,
And discovered the exit from the mind's maze.

A bird, as an egg, is first born;
It hatches — soon to be airborne.
Likewise is a human's birth,
Born in the shell of ignorance first,
Then breaks free — and forever quenches the thirst.

In Tune with Nature's Law

The law of the land is at times partial,
But isn't Nature's law ever impartial?
To get a judge's justice, someone may fail;
Then, doesn't the law of Nature prevail?

One may be master of one's mind,
Yet when he breaks her law, isn't he fined?
The law protects him who protects it —
Is one spared when he strays even a bit?

Idle talk, gossip, abuse, and lying —
Aren't these *speeches* binding us from flying?
Stealing, infidelity, and intoxication —
Aren't these *actions* halting our elevation?

Any *livelihood* can be a noble profession,
When practiced with moral discretion.
If a doctor wishes the disease to spread,
With a smiling face, does he go to bed?

Right speech, right action, right livelihood —
Aren't these steps toward sainthood?
Who guards these three with utmost care,
Is he not training the mind to be aware?

Nature's laws are simple yet deep:
"What you sow, so shall you reap!"
Abiding by this law, we do no one a favor;
In tune with Nature's law, we taste life's true flavor.

The Ultimate Journey — Beyond Nature

Drop by drop, the ocean is made;
So is awareness, with breathing's aid.
Feeling the breath entering and leaving,
With attention on a spot — keep perceiving.

Moment to moment — awareness of respiration,
The mind becomes focused, free from temptation.
Continuity of awareness is the secret to success;
To the unconscious level, one gains access.

Awareness is a faculty of the mind;
With constant practice, it is refined.
It serves as a loyal friend in times of need —
A guide on the path of truth, indeed.

Sustained awareness leads to concentration;
On the spot, one begins to feel some sensation —
Tingling, vibration, or subtle pulsation.

The task is to observe them as they are — without reaction.

The attention is then shifted away from the spot;
It is moved systematically from head to toes, ignoring each thought.
Observe sensations wherever attention is brought;
"Observe the reality as it is", is what Buddha taught.

Sensations are a mind-matter interaction;
Perceive their changing nature with conviction.
All sensations and reactions are impermanent;
To progress, equanimity is the determinant.

Equanimity is another faculty of the mind —
A measure of balance and purity combined.
Vicissitudes of life are bound to come;
Awareness and equanimity ensure a happy outcome.

Suffering piles up from entertaining thoughts;
Liberation is through untying the knots.
At a stage, the body is felt as a flow of vibration,
Continue observing to experience mind-matter cessation.

Disclaimer:

This poem is not a practice guide. The technique of Vipassana meditation is taught in a ten-day residential course. Visit www.dhamma.org to locate a centre nearest to you.

www.ingramcontent.com/pod-product-compliance
Lightning Source LLC
Chambersburg PA
CBHW070041070426
42449CB00012BA/3126